1987

SOCIAL WORK FIELD INSTRUCTION

The Undergraduate Experience

Richard Blake, Ph.D., ACSW
University College – Newark
Rutgers, The State University of New Jersey

Phylis J. Peterman, ACSW
Newark College of Arts and Sciences
Rutgers, The State University of New Jersey

With a foreword by
Carel B. Germain, ACSW, DSW

UNIVERSITY
PRESS OF
AMERICA

LANHAM • NEW YORK • LONDON

Copyright © 1985 by

University Press of America,® Inc.

4720 Boston Way
Lanham. MD 20706

3 Henrietta Street
London WC2E 8LU England

Library of Congress Cataloging in Publication Data

Blake, Richard.
   Social work field instruction.

   Includes bibliographies and index.
   1. Social service—Field work.   2. Social workers,
Professional ethics for.   I. Peterman, Phylis J.
II. Title.
HV11.B593   1985   361.3'07'11073   85-17907
ISBN 0-8191-4943-8 (alk. paper)
ISBN 0-8191-4944-6 (pbk. : alk. paper)

All University Press of America books are produced on acid-free
paper which exceeds the minimum standards set by the National
Historical Publications and Records Commission.

To the students and field
supervisors whose dedication has
inspired us over the years.

iii

CONTENTS

Preface

The primary objectives of this book are to introduce, orient, guide, and support upper - level undergraduate social work students with regard to the field practice component of their education and training. The book emerged from our experiences with field instruction at University College - Newark and Newark College of Arts and Sciences, Rutgers - The State University of New Jersey.

This student guide is not designed as a replacement for field manuals developed and used by individual baccalaureate social work programs. Rather, it is a supplement to these materials providing additional information and insights which are useful to students. Key issues are presented which are universally pertinent to undergraduate students.

Although the book is designed primarily for use by students, college administrators and faculty, as well as professionals in practice who accept responsibilities for supervising students, should find the materials useful.

Several of our colleagues provided advice and suggestions regarding the manuscript. We especially would like to thank Anne Adams of Rutgers University, Ida Eiger of Kean College, and Emma Quartero of Seton Hall University for their contributions. Of course, we alone are responsible for any shortcomings in the materials.

We would also like to thank our spouses, Laurie and Carl, for their insights and patience.

Richard Blake

Phylis J. Peterman

vii

Foreword

Field instruction is a major element in the education of the baccalaureate social worker. It provides a laboratory for the application of professional values and knowledge that are learned in the academic courses. As a laboratory, it is the means by which students develop and refine their professional skills, achieve the desired level of self-awareness, and integrate the knowing, feeling, and doing demands of social work practice. So it is not surprising that many students assess the field area of the curriculum as the most significant part of their professional education.

Blake and Peterman have written a book that will enhance the student's field experience still further, by helping to prepare them for the opportunities and pressures of field education. The book introduces students to the complexity of being learners and practitioners at the same time. And it helps to clarify the sometimes puzzling ambigious relationships to clients, field instructor and other agency personnel, and faculty advisor.

Most undergraduate programs in social work have developed field manuals or orientation programs for students as they enter their field placements. Field manuals, however, may focus only on policies and regulations. And experience suggests that the information conveyed during orientation, when one is both hopeful and anxious about the unknown experience ahead, is often not fully assimilated. Hence this book is designed to supplement such efforts, and it will be a welcome source of knowledge and reassurance to students as they seek to meet their practice tasks throughout their field experience.

Classroom instructors and their educational part-
ners - agency field instructors and administrators-
will find the book helpful in their own work with
students and in understanding the objectives and content of the field instruction in undergraduate social
work education.

Carel B. Germain, ACSW, DSW
Professor of Social Work
The University of Connecticut
School of Social Work

Chapter One

The Need for Practical Experience

Historically, formal preparation for social work practice began in 1898 in a summer training program sponsored by the New York Charity Organization Society. Through the first half of the twentieth century however, this preparation emerged as a function of many colleges and universities in the form of Masters degree programs and some undergraduate course offerings. During the 1960's the profession gave considerable thought regarding the education and training of practitioners and the needs of clients. As a result of these deliberations, persons holding a baccalaureate degree in social work were to be considered professionals and given the right to become full members in the National Association of Social Workers (NASW - the professional social work organization with 100,000 members in 1985). This action helped spawn the growth of undergraduate social work education programs in many colleges. In 1975 undergraduate degree programs in social work were eligible for accreditation by the Council on Social Work Education (CSWE). By 1985, there were three hundred and forty-seven accredited undergraduate social work degree programs and five awaiting accreditation.

With the institutionalization of undergraduate degree programs as the beginning level of professional social work practice, NASW established a classification system for persons involved in the provision of social services. This typology for practice delineates the minimum educational and experiential requirements for various social work tasks. According to NASW, a person holding an undergraduate degree in social work, under supervision, should be able to:

Provide social work services directed to specific, limited goals;

Conduct workshops to promote and interpret

1

programs or services;

Organize local community groups and coordinate their efforts to alleviate social problems;

Consult with other agencies on problems of cases served in common and coordinate services among agencies helping multiproblem families;

Conduct basic data-gathering or statistical analysis of data on social problems;

Develop information to assist legislators and other decision makers to understand problems and community needs;

Serve as an advocate of those clients or groups of clients whose needs are not being met by available programs or by a specific agency;

Work with groups to assist them in defining their needs or interests and in deciding on a course of action; and

Administer units of a program within an overall structure.(1)

The education and training of undergraduate students must prepare them for these types of tasks.

Social work is a professional activity, and as such, its practitioners must understand theories and be skillful in their application. They must be educated and trained. The training aspects of social work preparation are conducted to a large extent in social services agencies where students practice under the supervision of experienced professionals.

William E. Gordon and Margaret Shutz Gordon have presented a frame of reference which articulates three kinds of learning to be accomplished in preparation for social work practice:

Knowing - refers entirely to the cognitive realm and specifically to conceptual mastery of knowledge, to acquisition of constructs, generalizations, and concepts;

Understanding - refers to the ability to explain, to suggest what to look for further, to interpret, and to articulate expectations; and

Doing - refers to performance, activities which are recognized by others, acting on one's surroundings.(2)

Field experience refers to a learning situation in which students apply knowledge to actual client situations. It is designed largely to facilitate the doing aspects of becoming a social worker. Through field experience, students are helped to be prepared to carry out the purposes of social work: (a) to enhance the problem-solving, coping, and developmental capacities of people; (b) to promote the effective and humane operation of the systems that provide people with resources and services; and (c) to link people with systems that provide them with resources and opportunities.(3)

ORGANIZATION OF THE FIELD EXPERIENCE

As part of their educational experience, undergraduate students are required to complete at least three hundred hours of supervised practice experience in an actual social agency setting.(4) These hours can be structured into the total college program in various ways. Block instruction refers to an arrangement in which students participate in a series of academic courses over some period of time, followed by a full-time internship in a social services agency over another period of time. Although block instruction is a useful device for structuring the use of time, most undergraduate social work educational programs utilize the concurrent scheduling model. Under this system, students take some form of social work methods courses, an academic-field practice integration seminar of some form, and participate as interns in social services agencies during the academic year. For example, students may attend college classes on Monday, Tuesday, and Thursday and participate in the field experience on Wednesday and Friday. In addition to social work courses the senior year is also devoted to completion of other college requirements for graduation. Prior to the senior year, students take a series of general college and social work courses, including some form of

3

introductory field experience in many schools.

Whether or not the field experience is provided concurrently, in block form, or in some variation or combination of these depends upon the educational philosophy of the college as well as the faculty, agency, professional, student, and economic resources available to it. Undergraduate educational programs may be structured into colleges and universities as autonomous departments, such as a Department of Social Work, as components of other departments, such as Department of Sociology, Anthropology, and Social Work, or as undergraduate units of Schools of Social Work which offer Masters, and often Doctoral, levels of education. No matter what the structure, model, or relationship of the program to the college, the four year course of study is quite rigorous.

The field experience component of the educational program is designed to provide students with opportunities to integrate and utilize knowledge in a skillful manner. It usually consists of the student being placed in one community-based social services agency over the course of an academic year. At the agency the student learns and practices under the tutelage, guidance, and supervision of one professional who is employed by the respective agency. Although other arrangements may be used by different schools for different reasons, the preceding is generally applicable.

A successful field experience must have a framework or guidelines which explain that which is to be learned and mastered within some time period. The framework should provide clear expectations for student performance and should provide students with opportunities to practice skills and demonstrate that they have gained knowledge, understanding, and skill mastery. Dwyer and Urbanowski have articulated five major components of such framework, thus establishing, within reasonably wide parameters, that which is to be taught and learned.

Student Functioning Within the Service Delivery System and Various Environmental Systems- how and why the agency operates and its relationships to the community;

Student Functioning With the Client System: Use of the Scientific Method of Problem Solving on a Broad Range of Interventive Ap-- proaches in the Field Placement - the ability to understand the needs of clients and engage them in a successful helping process;

Student Functioning as a Learner: Use of Field Instructor, Pertinent Others, and Self in the Learning Process - taking responsibility for one's own learning:

Student Functioning in the Evaluation Process; Identifying Patterns of Learning, Working Through Learning Obstacles, and Recognizing Special Skills and Areas to be Developed - the ability to transfer learning from one situation to another; to identify problems in learning and invest in working through difficulties; and

Student Functioning as a Member of the Profession; Commitment to the Values and Basic Principles of the Profession and to Continued Education - a commitment to the values and ethical principles of the profession as guides to behavior and life-long learning.(5)

Although this framework lacks specificity and is somewhat general, this is understandable when one considers the broad array of settings in which social workers function. The field experience must help prepare students for the performance of professional functions in a wide variety of contexts.

In addition to serving as a guide for teaching and learning, frameworks such as the above help provide a structure for evaluating students performance, field supervisors abilities, and respective agencies as settings for education and training.

GOALS OF THE FIELD EXPERIENCE

Although field experience has been institutionalized in masters level social work educational programs for over fifty years, the development and proliferation of undergraduate programs since the late 1960's has brought new challenges to the profession. A basic issue, particularly relevant to baccalaureate programs, was presented in 1965 by Shubert who questioned whether

5

the educational objectives of the field experience should focus on skills in practice or knowledge about practice.(6) That is, should formal education focus on skills and techniques or should it be primarily involved with transmitting theoretical knowledge which can be put into practice subsequent to the formal learning experience. Although there has been, and continues to be, considerable debate within the profession concerning professional skills and baccalaureate level education and training (7), the major thrust of the field experience is to help students make skillful, humanistic use of knowledge. The field experience in social work is somewhat similar to internships in professions such as teaching and nursing in this regard.

A field placement in a social services agency should offer a student a stimulating exposure to professional social work practice. He or she will be exposed, through supervision, observation, and formal and informal observations and interaction, to professional role models. It is expected that students begin to become socialized into the profession, internalizing its characteristic ways of thinking and behaving. It is expected that students begin to develop a professional self-concept.

Not all students are transformed into professionals however. Field instruction also serves as a screening device for entry into the profession. Dawson has noted that there are many undergraduate students who can perform intellectually in class, but who cannot handle the realities of job pressures, client systems, relationship involvements, and the disciplined use of self required of social workers.(8) While such students often self-select themselves out of pursuing a career in social work or are advised against pursuing this goal by faculty members who are familiar with them, nevertheless, the field experience often serves a screening function for the profession by identifying students who are unable, for a variety of reasons, to handle the intellectual and emotional responsibilities of social work practice. Screening is an ancillary, unpleasant function of the field experience. Its primary mission is to help develop beginning level practitioners.

It is the responsibility of the agency field supervisor, in conjunction with academic faculty, to structure learning experiences in the agency in a cumulative, integrated manner, constantly building on what the student has previously learned and mastered. The intern enters the agency with some skills acquired over his or her lifetime. Learning experience at the social services agency are designed to build upon these and gradually develop the novice professionally over the course of the requisite three hundred hours.

Consider a student assigned to the social services department of a general hospital. Initially, the supervisor would examine referrals to the department and select an assignment which the student could satisfactorily complete. For example, the department has recently become aware that a patient requests information concerning local pharmacists who participate in the Medicaid program. The new intern would be given the requested information and asked to convey it to the patient. Over time, as the student gains confidence, knowledge, and mastery, her learning tasks might include learning the eligibility requirements for various social welfare programs; how to obtain referrals from other hospital professionals; how to make a psychosocial-medical assessment; how to develop a professional relationship with a client; and a host of other skills and social work functions. The key issue is that the learning is cumulative and practice experiences are designed to build upon that which the student has already learned and mastered.

The field experience is designed to provide students with opportunities to examine their abilities and experiment in a supervised environment. Students are to be given assignments which help them to learn; which are appropriate in terms of their emerging competencies; and which provide them a sense of satisfaction and accomplishment.

The field agency, however, exists to serve and meet the needs of clients; the needs of students are ancillary to this. The field experience involves working with real people who have real concerns, needs, and problems. It is important that students bring to the internship personal qualities such as intelligence, commitment to helping others, commitment to humanistic values, emotional responsiveness, enthusiasm and motivation, maturity and emotional stability, personal flexibility and openmindedness, a sense of caring, and a willingness to learn. The field agency is not an artificial laboratory for learning; it is a place where people go because they need help. Considering such, the student must at least have the aforementioned personal qualities to begin to be of service.

7

For many social work interns, field practice provides an awakening to the harsh realities endured by many people. Hunger is no longer an abstraction read about in the newspaper; the intern is faced with a client who has had nothing to eat for some time. Unemployment is no longer merely a statistic; the social worker stands face to face with someone who cannot find a job. Being frail and elderly no longer is something being pondered; the social worker meets with a group of senior citizens who are frightened. Child abuse no longer represents ugly pictures in the tabloids; a battered child is brought into the agency and the social worker must professionally respond.

These vignettes typify the types of situations the social work intern is called upon for intervention. In addition, the student is expected to conceptualize and formulate ideas concerning the underlying causes of social problems and consider what might be or ought to be available to people. Students are expected to intellectually and emotionally internalize the realities of social problems and learn how to respond professionally. This is a difficult task for the novice, indeed, it is a difficult task for experienced social workers.

Students are expected to be creative. Rarely is there an easy solution to problems. Very often the situations, concerns, and problems presented and endured by clients defy simple solutions. Social workers must therefore be thinking, creative people and training must challenge and encourage students in this regard.

Thinking and creativity require analytical reasoning and integration of knowledge from a range of subject areas and disciplines. It is for this reason that preparation for professional social work practice is provided within the broader system of higher education. As a professional, a student must not only be trained but also be liberally educated.

Considering the preceeding, Figure 1-1 is presented to illustrate the key elements involved in becoming a professional social worker.

Figure 1-1

BECOMING A SOCIAL WORKER

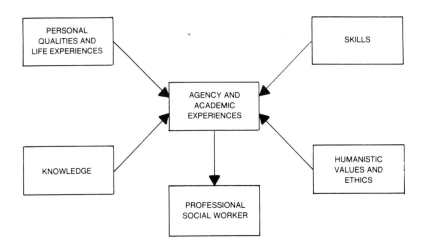

REFERENCES

1. <u>Standards for Social Service Manpower</u>. Washington, D.C., National Association of Social Workers, 1973.

2. Gordon, William E. and Gordon, Margaret Schutz: The role of frames of reference in field instruction. In Sheafor, Bradford W. and Jenkins, Lowell E.: <u>Quality Field Instruction in Social Work</u>. New York, Longman, 1982, pp. 21-36.

3. Baer, Betty L. and Federico, Ronald: <u>Educating the Baccalaureate Social Worker: Report of the Undergraduate Social Work Curriculum Project</u>. Cambridge, Ballinger, 1978, pp. 61-68.

4. <u>Standards For the Accreditation of Baccalaureate Degree Programs in Social Work (Effective July 1, 1974)</u>, New York, Council on Social Work Education, 74-210-19.

5. Dwyer, Margaret and Urbanowski, Martha: Field practice criteria: A valuable teaching/learning tool in undergraduate social work education. <u>Journal of Education for Social Work, 17</u>: pp. 5-11, Winter 1981.

6. Shubert, Margaret S.: Curriculum policy dilemmas in field instruction. <u>Journal of Education for Social Work, 1</u>: pp. 38-39, Fall 1965.

7. Alexander, Chauncey: The professional baccalaureate social worker. In Baer, Betty L. and Federico, Ronald C.: <u>Educating the Baccalaureate Social Worker: Report of the Undergraduate Social Work Curriculum Project</u>. Cambridge, Ballinger, 1978.

8. Dawson, Betty Guthrie: Supervising the undergraduate in a psychiatric setting. In <u>The Dynamics of Field Instruction: Learning Through Doing</u>. New York, Council on Social Work Education, 1975, pp. 10-19.

Chapter Two

Issues and Considerations - School, Agency, and Student

As presented in Chapter One, formal preparation for social work practice entails mutually agreed upon responsibilities of colleges, field agencies, field supervisors, and students. These educational elements are interrelated and interdependent. In Chapter Two basic issues which are especially pertinent to schools, agencies, and students are presented, followed by a discussion of supervision in Chapter Three.

THE SCHOOL

The educational program offered by the college should be accredited by the Council on Social Work Education (CSWE). A primary purpose of CSWE is to establish educational criteria and evaluate the degree to which respective college programs meet these criteria. At the baccalaureate level, educational criteria focus on what a beginning level social worker should know, understand, and be able to do. Considering such, accreditation is a form of quality assurance.

As a general rule, faculty in a social work educational program hold a Masters degree in social work and have had several years of practice experience. Increasingly, a doctoral degree in social work is being required for an academic position at the professorial level however.

In most undergraduate programs, at least one faculty member is specifically responsible for student field experiences. In other programs, faculty share this responsibility. Regardless of the administrative schema used by respective colleges, fieldwork administration is a difficult, demanding task.

A major responsibility of fieldwork administration is finding appropriate agency settings. Dinerman, in a study of professional social work education, found that selection of field placement sites generally involves agencies which are accessible to students and which are perceived as having the ability to provide meaningful learning experiences for students.(1) Accessibility of field agencies is a key issue which impacts upon administrative decisions at the college regarding block or concurrent scheduling of the course of study.

College faculty find field agency sites and supervisors through formal and informal means. Formally, faculty may correspond with community agencies, inquiring as to their willingness and suitability to serve students. Based on this correspondence, a formal dialogue may take place between faculty and agency personnel resulting in a contract regarding the education and training of students. As happens frequently, faculty and professionals in practice in the community tend to know of each other, and thus the initial phase of finding field training sites can be somewhat informal. It is expected that faculty and community practitioners know of each other; faculty are expected to be aware of the social services delivery system in the community served by the school; community practitioners depend upon schools for supplying staff and often have formal input into the college program by means of serving on an advisory board. In addition, faculty and community practitioners tend to know each other through membership and participation in various professional organizations, task forces, and committees. Colleges and social services agencies often are linked through the outreach of the latter. Agencies and potential field supervisors often contact schools to inquire about the availability of student interns. In addition, students suggest their own field agency sites at times.

After establishing the viability of social services agencies as field training sites, the faculty person responsible for this aspect of education must link students with field agencies.

In linking students with agencies, college faculty may be faced with a dilemma brought on by the reality that some agencies and supervisors have greater ability to serve the needs of students than others. In addition, some students are more motivated and have demonstrated greater affinity for social work practice than others. The dilemma concerns who should be linked with whom. Contributing to the dilemma is the fact that

12

college enrollments for students majoring in social work have been declining.(2) Consequently, there may be some pressure on colleges to retain some students who might have been advised to discontinue their studies in the past. The dilemma may be exacerbated by recent reductions in social welfare expenditures which have caused some agencies to reduce staff and services. As a result, supervision of students may be considered a luxury an agency cannot afford. Students may be considered more for their ability to render services to clients then for their own educational needs. These are serious issues in social work education today requiring professionalism and commitment to ethical principles. These issues impact heavily upon the faculty person whose task is to link students with agencies.

It is imperative that college faculty have working knowledge about the field agency - its clients, service area, service offerings, and so forth. It is also imperative that faculty know each student - abilities, learning needs, transportation needs, and so forth. It is through this type of detailed knowledge and understanding of respective agencies and students that appropriate placements can be facilitated.

A useful device for linking students and field agencies is to have students who are completing their field experience meet with those who have yet to begin. In this way students themselves share information and incoming students are given another perspective regarding the experience. Another useful device is to have potential field supervisors and students meet as a group prior to formal arrangements. Through group and individual interaction, students may develop an interest in certain agencies. Most often, however, the process is negotiated and consumated by faculty meeting with students on an individual basis to discuss and plan field training sites, followed by students and agency personnel interviewing each other. Usually, faculty have materials in print regarding various agencies which students are encouraged to peruse to help with the decision.

Another major responsibility of the college program involves <u>articulation and clarification of the rights and responsibilities</u> of the school, agency, supervisor, and student. This usually takes the form of a contract and fieldwork manual which is distributed to supervisors and students. College faculty develop their respective manuals using educational materials developed by the Council on Social Education, their own knowledge and insights, and contributions from supervisors and students over the years.

The fieldwork manual is an indispensible tool for guiding the field experience. It must be specific yet have provisions which allow for the individual needs of students and agencies. The fieldwork manual should introduce the student to the field experience; state the objectives of teaching - learning experiences in behavioral terms; describe the various types of agencies used as placement sites; identify the professionals who function as supervisors; elucidate the respective responsibilities of the college, agency, supervisor, and student; contain guidelines concerning evaluation processes, including copies of formal evaluative instruments used; and contain other pragmatic information which each college may deem important.

The fieldwork manual helps to minimize the potential for problems to emerge over the semester; nevertheless, problems do emerge at times. Problems related to student attendance, performance, and so forth are sometimes voiced by individual supervisors about individual students. At times students voice concerns about assignments, quality and quantity of supervision, and a host of other issues. Although students and supervisors often resolve these issues between themselves, a responsibility of faculty is to intervene and mediate in the event there are unresolved problems regarding a student, supervisor, or agency. If it is not possible to resolve such a problem, or if it is deemed to be in the best interests of the parties, students may be transferred to another agency or supervisor.

Professionals in agencies who function as field supervisors often require training and assistance in their teaching role. This is particularly relevant for professionals who have never supervised a baccalaureate level student. College faculty have responsibility for providing training, assistance, and consultation to supervisors when necessary. These activities can be carried out with supervisors on an individual or group basis. The key issue is that it cannot be assumed that because a person has professional knowledge and skills that this person automatically can teach students.

Consultation with field supervisors also provides a mechanism for college faculty to learn and consider changes in their curriculum. Faculty are responsible for keeping abreast of new developments, theories, and

so forth and interaction with community practitioners .
is one means whereby this may be achieved.

During the academic year faculty meet with students regularly on an individual and/or group basis to
discuss progress, issues, and learning experiences. In
addition, faculty also meet periodically with individual supervisors to discuss the performance and
learning needs of individual students. It is helpful if
students participate, to some extent, in these discussions as the learning endeavor involves mutual responsibilities and all parties should be open and honest
with each other and acting on similar information.

From the college's perspective, fieldwork is ex-
pensive. The aforementioned responsibilities of faculty
dictate a relatively low student-teacher ratio. In
addition, there are considerable expense items such as
telephone, mail, printing, and faculty transportation
involved with operating a social work program.

Fieldwork responsibilities often place a strain on
faculty who must also meet traditional academic requirements. Colleges require faculty to be active with
regard to scholarly research, publications, advisement,
teaching, professional and community service, and serving on college committees. The strains associated with
these responsibilities may be heightened somewhat in
smaller social work programs were faculty have multiple
responsibilities regarding the curriculum. Two-thirds
of independent (not affiliated with a graduate program)
undergraduate social work programs have four or less
full-time faculty.(3)

The Practice Seminar

Most undergraduate social work programs require
students to participate in a seminar which is taken
concurrently with the field experience. The seminar
usually meets on a regularly scheduled basis and brings
together a small group of students with a member of the
college faculty.

A major objective of the seminar is to strengthen
the relationship between academic course content from a
variety of subject areas and the field practice
experience. Considering such, the faculty member must
be knowledgeable about a variety of subject areas;
knowledgeable about specific types of social work

practice; knowledgeable about a variety of practice settings and; knowledgeable about the total social work curriculum. In addition to being knowledgeable about many facets of social work education and practice, the faculty member must have the ability to help students integrate the total learning experience.

In the small group setting students are expected to be verbal, articulate, and willing to share thoughts, feelings, and experiences. The faculty member must have the ability to facilitate discussion and encourage people to speak. Most often a problem-centered approach is used as the basis for discussions. A problem-centered approach requires that students present actual client situations in terms of causes, manifestations, intervention techniques, and a host of other issues. Confidentiality, of course, is maintained in these discussions.

The practice seminar helps to socialize students into the profession. There is mutual sharing of insights and feelings in an atmosphere more personal and informal than that usually encountered in a typical college course. The seminar serves to help students present themselves and client situations in a professional manner. It is designed to foster clarity of expression.

Considering that undergraduate students usually fulfill the requirements for field experience at one specific agency, there is some danger that they may learn well how to function in this particular agency but have little confidence in their ability to function in a different setting. The seminar addresses this issue by exposing students to issues and perspectives which are common to the practice of all social workers. The seminar enables students to learn about various types of social work practice and settings and helps them consider the type of practice they would like to enter after graduation.

Another function of the field practice seminar is to identify and help clarify issues and problems which may emerge in the field experience. Even though social work educational programs have a fieldwork manual and the field experience is based upon a mutually agreed upon contract, nevertheless, issues, problems, and ambiguities often arise during the semester and these are often identified and resolved early during sessions of the practice seminar.

THE AGENCY

Students learn in a variety of formally organized settings. Usually these are social services agencies which provide services that people need, yet can't obtain by means of the free market system for a variety of reasons. These agencies may be operated by various levels of government or be private, non-profit in nature and they exist to ameliorate or prevent social problems and their effects on people. In addition to these types of agencies, social work activities often are carried out in other organizations whose express purposes may not be provision of social work services per se. These would include hospitals, nursing homes, schools, jails, and others.

A recent study of the membership of the National Association of Social Workers revealed the following practice areas in which social workers function:

Practice Area	Percentage of Membership Reporting
Children and Youth	15.5
Community Organizing	1.8
Family Services	11.2
Criminal Justice	1.7
Group Services	0.4
Medical or Health Care	18.1
Mental Health	26.6
Public Assistance	1.0
School Social Work	3.4
Services to Aged	4.5
Alcohol/Drug/Substance Abuse	2.9
Mental Retardation	3.2

(continued)

Other Disabilities	0.5	
Occupational	0.4	
Combined Areas	4.8	
Other	4.0	(4)
	100.0	

Although there is variety in the profession as illustrated above, not all social work settings are available or applicable to undergraduate students. The uniqueness of a particular region and the service area of the college also act as constraints on the availability of field practice settings. Some types of agencies may not be available in a college's service area. In addition, some practice settings are inappropriate for baccalaureate level practice and training. Undergraduate education and training prepares students for beginning level professional practice. Provision of psychotherapy services and college instruction are clearly not beginning level areas of practice and hence are inappropriate for baccalaureate field learning purposes. Complicating matters further is the fact that some types of agencies provide a broad range of services, and provision of some of these may be beyond the expected capacities of undergraduate students. In a general hospital for example, discharge planning may be an appropriate undergraduate learning experience while working with a mother who is ambivalent about allowing her newborn to be adopted would not be. With other settings, the issues are not as clear as those presented above. Although the National Association of Social Workers has articulated functional differences between the various levels of social work preparation and experience (5), in practice the issues remain somewhat vague and complicated.

It is not necessary for agencies to employ BSW level staff, nor to have specific entry level job descriptions in order to serve as field learning sites. Whether or not a specific agency is willing to accept baccalaureate students for training, and a college is willing to place students there, depends upon several factors including:

The degree of complexity involved with completion of typical agency tasks;

The philosophy of the agency with regard to BSW level activities;

Previous experiences of the agency with BSW students;

Previous experiences of the college with the agency;

The mission and philosophy of the college program;

Licensing and regulatory constraints on the provision of various types of services by state governments;

The abilities of respective students being considered for placement; and

The degree to which respective agencies can provide meaningful learning experiences to students.

The phrase meaningful learning experiences is an issue requiring further explication.

Agencies, for the most part, provide specific, limited types of services; have specific missions or purposes; and have specific criteria concerning selection and acceptance of clients. Considering such, knowledge which is specific to a particular agency is required in order to function in that agency. Consequently, a student in a hospital will gain knowledge and understanding specifically pertinent to social work practice in hospitals; a student in a correctional facility will gain knowledge and understanding pertinent to social work practice in the field of corrections; and so forth.

It is extremely important that students do not confuse means with ends regarding specific knowledge they gain during the field experience. Students need specific knowledge and understanding pertinent to respective agencies in order to learn to use themselves in a helping process. After graduation they may become employed in other types of agencies and will learn and use specific knowledge and understanding applicable to that particular agency and client group. Therefore, students must be able to transfer what has been learned in one setting to another. It is the responsibility of the school, the agency, the supervisor, and the student to accomplish this. In other words, interns are not

19

trained to function in X Hospital or Y Community Agency, but rather, are to be trained to function as professional social workers and the particular agency, with its specific knowledge and understanding requirements, is the laboratory for this purpose. A meaningful learning experience is one which prepares students for this transfer of learning.

There are other important concerns pertaining to the service limitations of agencies and the social workers who practice in them. Teare and McPheeters have identified twelve roles which are carried out in social work practice: (6)

Outreach worker - involves efforts aimed at locating people who may be eligible for a service, informing them about the service, and assisting them to utilize the service;

Broker - linking people with programs and services to which they may be entitled, information and referral services;

Advocate - interceding on behalf of people who have inappropriately been denied services and benefits, activities aimed at making more programs and services available to more people;

Mobilizer - activities involved with bringing people together to effect some change in their social environment;

Behavior changer - helping people to understand the consequences of their actions and helping them alter their behavior;

Teacher - showing people how to help themselves in a variety of situations;

Care giver - helping people to do things which they are unable to do for themselves, acting in a supportive manner;

Consultant - working with other professionals and agencies in an effort to help them be more effective;

Community planner - assessing the needs of a community and evaluating various ways of meeting these needs;

20

Data manager - activities involved with managing information;

Administrator - functioning in a position of formal authority in an agency; and

Evaluator - assessing the consequences of various actions and proposed actions.

Professional staff in social services agencies usually are engaged in a limited number of these roles, yet students need experience with as many possible. A meaningful field experience offers students practice experiences in at least several of these roles and helps them conceptualize what they are doing and why. In order to maximize the learning experience, agencies and supervisors often have to seek out experiences pertaining to the roles identified above. This special effort exemplifies commitment to education and training.

A meaningful field learning experience is one in which the agency provides a positive educational climate. It is one in which the student is given a place of importance and is provided with the physical amenities necessary to facilitate learning such as a desk, space in which to work, and so forth. As noted earlier, there may be potential for some agencies to seek out students more for the additional service help they provide than for their learning needs. Although there is a trade-off of sorts, since the student does function in a service capacity while he or she is learning, these agencies are inappropriate for learning.

A positive educational climate is one which helps nurture a questioning mentality in the student. Students should feel comfortable asking questions about what they have seen and done. This is a major reason why students are usually discouraged from using their place of employment, if pertinent, as a field learning setting. There is role strain associated with this type of arrangement as expectations for employees are different from expectations for students. Agencies pay a salary and expect employees to perform; students are also expected to perform but their performance is related to learning more than to service delivery per se. Using employment settings as field learning agencies for individual students presents students with little recourse if assignments and experiences are not appropriate.

Students usually begin the field experience with excitement, interest, and some apprehension. At the beginning students should receive information about the agency concerning its goals, services offered, clientele served, personnel, personnel policies, and community resources. They should be given a tour of the agency and be introduced to other staff. Students should also be shown the types of records kept by the agency and given some exposure to the various forms, applications, and so forth.

Although this type of orientation is helpful at the start, it should not be used to unnecessarily delay interaction with clients. The longer the delay in interacting with clients, the more anxious students are likely to become and this can be a real hindrance to learning. This presents an educational dilemma. Students are asked to intervene with clients before they are sufficiently prepared, yet they can't be sufficiently prepared without actually engaging themselves with clients over time. The answer to this dilemma lies in the appropriateness of assignments. Students come to agencies with some communication and writing skills. They should initially be given assignments which help them use what they have already mastered in life. Assignments should then become more complex as the novice gains knowledge, understanding, skill mastery, and confidence.

By the midpoint of the field experience students should be able to describe and analyze their respective agency. Again, it is to be noted that the field agency serves as a laboratory for learning. Students are not merely expected to be able to describe a particular agency, but rather are expected to use the agency experience to help them learn to examine programs and organizations analytically. Besides knowing who is served by their respective agency, students should also understand the implications of who is not served and why; what services do clients need which are not available and how might provision of these services become a reality.

Other matters which are important for students to understand and be able to analyze include:

history of the agency;

agency goals, including how and why goals may have changed over time;

the degree to which agency goals are met, including student suggestions for improving the agency;

services offered and techniques used at the agency;

client, staff, and community involvement in decision making;

client, staff, and community attitudes toward the agency;

demographic characteristics of clients served;

relationship of the agency to the network of agencies in the community;

sources of agency funding;

agency personnel practices;

implications regarding practicing in a bureaucracy;

influence of local and national economic climate on agency service delivery;

agency organization chart; and

overall agency strengths and weaknesses, including recommendations for change and improvement.

THE STUDENT

Efforts and activities by the college and field agency are designed to <u>help students help themselves learn</u>.

It is expected that students begin and end the field experience with enthusiasm and a strong desire to learn and grow professionally. At the beginning, many students feel a moderate amount of stress. They ask themselves questions such as "Have I made a correct career decision?"; "Will I be able to help others?"; "Will I be treated fairly at the agency?"; and a host of other questions. Faculty and supervisors are expected to be sensitive to these concerns. Students are in a new environment, and are relatively unclear as to what they will be asked to do and their ability to meet demands.

These stresses should gradually disappear over time as interns get used to their surroundings and are given practical assignments which are possible for them to satisfactorily complete. Stresses which continue should be discussed with the supervisor and/or college faculty. A delay in discussing problems may diminish the total learning experience.

There are other pressures felt by students in addition to those associated with entry into a new environment. The typical undergraduate student beginning the field experience is a twenty-one year old college senior. Without implying a generalized lack of maturity to people in this age group, it seems reasonable that based on age alone, many students may have had relatively limited opportunities for acting in an adult role. The field agency not only offers opportunity for acting in an adult role but demands it. Younger students may feel stresses associated with carrying serious responsibilities at the agency which may not be reinforced in other environments such as home or with friends.

There has been discussion about this issue within the profession. Some agencies and supervisors will not accept undergraduate students for training yet they will accept first-year graduate students who have little or no social work background. Those who take this position feel that graduate level students are somewhat older, have made a more serious educational commitment, and hence are more appropriate for professional training. While it is true that graduate level students are typically older than undergraduate students, and graduate level education does represent a serious commitment, undergraduate professional training is necessary and viable. Undergraduate education is also a serious undertaking and college seniors are adults. From a pragmatic point of view, many employment opportunities in social welfare are available to college graduates. It seems reasonable to assert that if one is ready for employment at the end of college, one is ready for education and training in college. If a person is unable to handle the responsibilities of field practice he or she must be counseled out of the educational program.

The college curriculum is designed to help ensure that students are prepared to begin the field experience. Majoring in social work is more than the accumulation of some requisite number of college credits; the student also undergoes a transformation into a professional. The curriculum serves to socialize students into the profession and course offerings are designed to be cumulative in nature. Considering such, a student cannot decide to major in social work in September and enroll in all social work course offerings over the academic year in order to graduate in May. He and she must have satisfactorily completed some course work before beginning the field experience. This helps faculty know the student to some degree and ensures that the student has been exposed to portions of the social work knowledge base as well as the value system of social work practice.

Education and training for the profession is a process requiring active participation on the part of the learner. In some college courses, students attend lectures, complete assigned readings, write term papers, and pass examinations. This represents what is known as passive learning. In social work education, particularly the field learning component, the student must be an active learner. Students are expected to be vocal, to ask questions, to discuss their feelings about the services they are providing and the methodologies being used, and to actively seek out new responsibilities. This requires that they be self-aware, self-directed, and open to new ideas. Active learning takes place at the school, at the agency, and with peers. Despite the best efforts of college faculty and agency supervisors, it is students themselves who must consciously think about what they are doing, why,

25

and how the various knowledge components of social work practice apply to various situations.

REFERENCES

1. Dinerman, Miriam: Social Work Curriculum at the Baccalaureate and Masters Levels. New York, The Lois and Samuel Silberman Fund, 1981, p. 58.

2. Rubin, Allen: Statistics on Social Work Education in the United States: 1982. New York, Council on Social Work Education, 1983, p. 28. With the assistance of Denise Waterman.

3. Dinerman, Miriam: op. cit., p. 62.

4. NASW News, 28: 10 November 1983, p. 6.

5. Standards for Social Service Manpower. Washington, D.C., National Association of Social Workers, 1973.

6. Teare, Robert and McPheeters, Harold: Manpower Utilization in Social Welfare. Atlanta, Southern Regional Education Board, 1970, pp. 34-35.

Chapter Three

Supervision

In social agencies, social work students learn and function under the guidance of a competent professional, who is generally referred to as the student's supervisor.

As used by the general public, the term "supervisor" usually refers to a bureaucratic functionary who has responsibility for the performance of other employees. Thus conceived, the supervisory role is largely administrative in nature and helps ensure effectiveness and efficiency in the operation of organizations. To varying degrees such supervisors may also carry responsibilities for the training and development of those for whom they are responsible in the bureaucratic hierarchy. In social work, however, particularly with regard to students and those with limited practice experience, the supervisory role is primarily educative in nature. Supervision is a proud tradition of social work.

THE STRUCTURE OF SUPERVISION

Although the term supervisor is used throughout this book, some college programs refer to agency professionals who train students as field faculty or some other title. Regardless of the term used in reference to them, these social work practitioners play a major role in the education and training of students.

Supervision is designed to offer the student face to face exchanges with an experienced practitioner over an extended period of time. While a variety of possible supervisory models exist, such as group supervision, combined individual and group supervision, and consultant supervision, the frame of reference used in this chapter is the traditional one to one relationship

27

between student and professional. The materials presented however are applicable to the broad range of supervisory models.

The person to whom responsibility is given for agency-based education and training must be a competent, experienced professional. Usually this refers to a person who has completed masters level education at a CSWE accredited college and who has been in practice for at least two years. At times however there are people, not formally trained in social work, who provide social welfare services in agencies. Disciplines such as certain fields of psychology, applied sociology, urban studies, public administration, and others are related to social work. In the absence of specific state licensing requirements to the contrary, people with education in these disciplines may be employed in social agencies. These persons may be quite knowledgeable and effective in their particular job. If a college program is faced with constraints regarding the availability of professionally trained social workers to function as supervisors, these other persons might be considered. It is to be noted however, that in these types of arrangements the school must also find some other way to ensure that students have exposure to and consultation with professionally trained social workers. While untrained personnel may be competent in various aspects of social service delivery, social work is a distinctive profession requiring that students receive distinctive education and training. Particularly considering that the supervisor serves as a role model for socializing students into the profession, it is expected that the supervisor is one who has been professionally trained in social work; use of others must be the exception rather than the rule.

As discussed earlier, it is recommmended that the student meet with the supervisor prior to formal assignment by the college. The supervisor should assume a leadership role in this process and should be aware of college requirements and the ability of the respective agency to facilitate meeting these requirements. During this initial interview the supervisor makes a relatively quick assessment of the student's suitability for the agency. In addition, the student is given information about the agency such as services offered, clients served, and so forth.

Potential interns must play an active role in this preliminary interview. They are responsible for assessing whether the agency and supervisor will meet their learning needs. Even though the college has selected various agencies to serve as training sites, it is the student himself who will function in these agencies and so it is the student's responsibility to take an active role during the initial interview.

Once the student has agreed to an agency and supervisor, and has been accepted by them, several things must be accomplished. Prior to the start of the training, students and supervisors should develop a contract with each other regarding mutual expectations. College faculty play a major role in arranging this contract, yet it is the student and the supervisor who must operationalize this agreement as they will be working with each other rather closely over an extended period of time.

Wilson notes that a contract is like a roadmap for the field experience.(1) It is a guide for articulating the goals and objectives, tasks, and responsibilities of each party. Due to potential for misunderstandings to arise, it is recommended that the contract be in writing, although care should be taken that the contracting process not be cold and impersonal. Over the course of the semester the contract may have to be altered for a variety of legitimate reasons - it is difficult to know in September what will be transpiring in February. Changes in the contract must be discussed by all parties and should also be in writing.

The contract should note the student's schedule in terms of hours to be spent each week at the agency in the traditional field arrangement. In addition, agreement should be reached regarding field agency responsibilities over college intersession periods. Many colleges do not conduct classes for extended periods of time during December and January. The student's responsibilities at the agency during this period should be included in the contract.

The contract should explicate the context for supervisory sessions - how both parties are to conduct themselves. In terms of time, as a general rule, students should receive about one hour of supervision each week and this period should be formally scheduled by both parties in most instances.

While use of a contract is important, discretion, spontaneity, and creativity are likewise important. The contract is a tool, not a master.

Students and supervisors are each responsible for preparing for supervisory sessions. A supervisor who begins sessions with comments such as "What would you like to discuss today?" is not prepared for supervision. Comments such as this represent "games" supervisors can play with students as a defense for being unprepared or ill at ease.(2) There are also a host of "games" which students can play in an effort to avoid serious, meaningful discussions with the supervisor.(3) The point is neither party is there to play games; both must make serious efforts to be self-aware, open and prepared in order to maximize the learning experience.

The supervisor is responsible for setting the climate for supervisory sessions. She must be accepting and help the student discuss activities, feelings, and ideas. An accepting attitude is conveyed by vocal intonation and body language. The student should be given a message that both she and what is being discussed is important. To facilitate this, the supervisor should make appropriate arrangements to ensure that there are no interruptions from others in the agency during supervisory sessions.

In some agency settings a supervisor may be able to see first-hand what and how a student is doing. These types of settings would include day programs for senior citizens, sheltered workshops, and other programs in which clients are seen, for the most part, in groups. In such a setting the supervisor's observations of the student's performance could be included in formal supervisory sessions, or sooner if necessary. In other settings, such as those which provide counseling services, where interaction between the student and the client is more on a one-to-one basis, the agenda for supervisory sessions must be based upon information and materials which the student and supervisor have devoted some thought and preparation. Considering such, the less the supervisor can see and hear client-student interactions directly, the more the student is required to present these interactions in written form prior to supervisory sessions. Written materials may include process notes, logs, summaries, or agency records. Preparation of written materials also helps students rethink what they have done and learn from their musings. Even though supervision is based on an agenda, sessions also require spontaneity and brainstorming on the part of the student and the supervisor.

The supervisor must plan and arrange for students to have appropriate assignments at the agency. An assignment or experience is appropriate if it offers the student a challenge; if the student can learn or gain practice experience from it and; if it offers the student good chances of success. Assignments must also be assessed in terms of consequences for clients, considering that the student is a novice. Obviously, the needs of clients take precedence over the learning needs of students. The supervisor must also carefully gauge the amount of time necessary to complete a task or assignment and the amount of time the student has available. Issues of time, as well as level of expertise of the student and typical presenting problems of clients, are decisive factors regarding the types of learning experiences available to students. For example, students should not be asked to intervene on Tuesday in situations which will probably require further intervention on Wednesday when they will not be at the agency.

Assignments can be relationship-centered or task-centered and these can be conceptualized as opposite ends of a continuum of direct service experiences. In the relationship-centered approach, a client is assigned to the student. Settings which may facilitate a relationship approach to practice would include, but not be limited to, prisons, schools, nursing homes, senior citizens programs, and others. In such programs, students learn how to develop a professional relationship with a client and they may have to assume a variety of roles in serving the client. In the task-centered approach, students are responsible for specific types of interventions as contrasted with ongoing client caseloads per se. Settings which seem applicable for task-approach experience would include, but not be limited to, agencies which provide concrete services such as entitlement benefits, charities, information and referral services, travelors' aid, and others. As a general rule, the more an agency is oriented toward providing short-term concrete services, the less opportunity students have for practicing the skill of forming and maintaining professional relationships. Both of these approaches are necessary in social work practice, and if possible, the supervisor should make learning assignments which give the student exposure to and experience with both.

THE SUPERVISOR AS TEACHER

A major function of social work supervision is teaching. Consequently, colleges make strong efforts to ensure that supervisors, in addition to being experienced practitioners, are good teachers. Particularly with regard to inexperienced supervisors, colleges usually sponsor seminars, meetings, and programs to help practitioners more adequately perform as teachers. The basic premise behind this is the notion that knowing something doesn't automatically mean that one can teach it to others. Teaching is both an art and a science. Considering its scientific aspects, it is important that supervisors understand, theoretically and practically, the prerequisites for learning and how people learn. This is the foundation for teaching.

Learning to be a social worker entails activity on the part of the student using a problem-solving approach with feedback and direction by the supervisor. It is generally agreed that feedback which is most useful is that which primarily builds on the student's strengths, rather than on correction of mistakes. At times, however, this latter approach may be necessary considering that students are working with clients in actual problem-solving situations.

Feedback from the supervisor should encourage the student to think. For example, the supervisor may ask the student "What options do you consider most viable for Mrs. S. and why?". The supervisor would then help the student think through various courses of action. Encouraging students to think helps them learn concepts as contrasted with a series of rote answers to various problem situations. It is conceptual learning which differentiates professions from other occupations. Conceptual learning helps the student transfer learning from one situation to another and helps to develop creativity, so necessary in professional social work practice. Conceptual learning leads to greater amounts of knowledge, accumulated more rapidly. Providing feedback to the student which is practical and theoretical helps the student to develop the capacity for scientific thinking and helps him or her become habituated to using and evaluating theories in relation to problematic social situations.

Feedback should be presented in language which the student understands. Even though a function of supervision is to socialize students into the profession -

it's characteristic ways of thinking, behaving, and speaking - care must be taken that students understand what is being spoken. Conversations which use language that flaunts the supervisor's authority, keeps the student at a distance, or which serves to camouflage the supervisor's insecurity or unpreparedness are inappropriate. The supervisor needs to be confident in her own competence and take a genuine interest in the student.

The supervisor has to assess the applicability of various techniques which help people learn and be competent in their application. These techniques include role playing, modeling, didactic explanation, group problem-solving, repetition and reinforcement, and presentation and analysis of case histories and other readings. In using various teaching techniques the supervisor informs, guides, and encourages the student. She is a facilitator, resource person, and mentor.

The supervisor must make sure that the student is given an appropriate amount of work. Having too many or too few clients to serve is frustrating for the learner. In making sure that assignments are appropriate in terms of level of skill and knowledge required for their completion, timing is an important consideration. The supervisor may have to wait until the student is ready before assigning certain types of learning experiences. This is because students do not learn in an ever increasing, steady manner as depicted below.

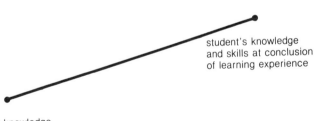

student's knowledge
and skills at conclusion
of learning experience

student's knowledge
and skills at beginning
of learning experience

Most often students learn as per the following model.

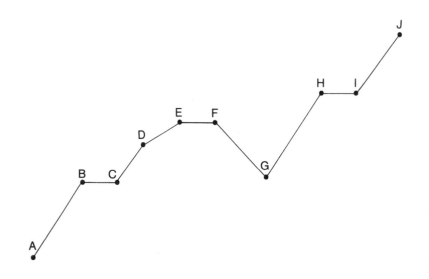

In the model depicted above, the length of lines AB, CD, DE, GH, and IJ depends upon the amount of information a student can absorb before he or she needs a mental rest in order to internalize and integrate it. The angle of these lines depends upon the difficulty of the material as experienced by the respective student. Lines BC, EF, and HI represent the length of time each student needs for internalization and integration before he or she is ready for new information. Line FG reflects a situation whereby the student may forget, regress, or become resistant to new information. Supervisors must be patient and understand this. Perhaps the student needs repetition and reinforcement or perhaps something else is happening in the student's life which is affecting his or her learning.

Point J above represents the level of knowledge and skill expected of the baccalaureate student at the completion of the formal learning experience. While there is considerable variability regarding students' abilities at the conclusion of the field experience, in order to graduate and begin employment as a beginning level social worker, each must know enough and be competent enough, with continued supervision on the job, to complete the types of responsibilities presented in Chapter One.

Learning to be competent enough to begin professional social work practice requires dedication and motivation. Students must be self-motivated and have a keen sense of responsibility for their own learning.

An effective supervisor is one who realizes that learning is an individual process and that there are influences and factors in each person's life which affect his or her ability to learn and grow. The supervisor should know something about the student as a person and this requires that the student be honest and open with her. This is not to imply prying, being nosey, overfocusing on the student's personality, or engaging in a form of psychotherapeutic relationship on the part of the supervisor. Actions such as these are not helpful and not within the purview of social work supervision. An effective supervisor is one who realizes that learning can be blocked by overly anxious feelings and who takes action to give the student support and encouragement. People learn with their feelings as well as their intellect.

REFERENCES

1. Wilson, Suanna: Field Instruction: Techniques for Supervisors. New York, The Free Press, 1981, p. 23

2. Hawthorne, Lillian: Games supervisors play. Social Work, 20: pp. 179-183, May 1975.

3. Kadushin, Alfred: Games people play in supervision. Social Work, 13: pp. 23-32, July 1968.

Chapter Four

Evaluation

THE STRUCTURE AND PROCESS OF EVALUATION

In traditional academic courses the degree to which a student has met course objectives is reflected in a grade which is assigned by a respective instructor. A similar process takes place with regard to the field learning experience, however the evaluation of the student is based upon measurement and appraisal of a more complicated range of knowledge, behaviors, and attitudes. Evaluation of field performance serves several purposes including:

identifying areas of student strengths and weaknesses in practice;

identifying how the student adjusts to changing, complex situations;

providing a reference guide for prospective employers and/or graduate schools;

promoting student growth; and

assessing the adequacy of the learning situation.

Kerrigan states that evaluation in social work education is a powerful definer of professional development.(1) It is a process which lasts from the first to the last assignment. Evaluation begins on the first day of the field experience, not at midterm, the end of the semester, or some other specific point in time. While a formal evaluation document or report may be prepared at such periodic intervals, the process of evaluation is ongoing and dynamic. For example, feedback from the supervisor during supervisory sessions is a form of evaluation.

Evaluations should be based on clear, observable, measurable criteria that are mutually understood and agreed upon by the student, supervisor and college faculty. When the student and the supervisor articulate a contract regarding their mutual responsibilities, they are agreeing to and establishing mechanisms for appraising the student's performance, as well as the agency's and supervisor's ability to facilitate the student's learning.

Students and supervisors should receive a copy of the formal evaluation document used by the college at the beginning of the field experience. The student must know at the start that for which he or she will be examined and graded. This aids in planning goals and articulating how these goals are to be met.

Agency supervisors are responsible for formally evaluating the performance of students and colleges set time deadlines for receipt of documentation regarding this performance. Formal evaluation at periodic intervals is an orderly, planned activity which should catch no one by surprise. Considering that evaluation is an ongoing process, the formal appraisal document should only include information which has been conveyed to and shared with the student prior to completion of the written report.

Wilson has offered a step by step guide for student evaluations which captures the main aspects of what is required of supervisors.(2) The agency supervisor should:

determine the student's level of functioning upon entering the agency;

determine what the student must learn and the best ways of teaching it;

establish the level of skill or competence the student must achieve in the desired areas;

determine how to monitor what the student is doing and apply appropriate methods for assessing performance;

determine the level of the student's

performance in relation to standards and expectations;

communicate to the student conclusions that have been reached;

put the evaluation into writing and share it with the student; and

deal with the student's reaction to the evaluation.

The evaluation is based upon the student's demonstrated knowledge and competence in several key areas.

The student must understand the organizational structure of his or her respective agency and the community in which it is located. With increased experience, exposure, and supervision, the student's knowledge, self-confidence, ability to function more independently, and willingness to question agency and governmental practices should increase and develop. At the conclusion of the field experience, the intern should exhibit development of skills of problem identification, collection, synthesis, and analysis of data and information, planning and implementation of intervention efforts, and evaluation of these intervention efforts. The student must understand the use of scientific methods of problem-solving and intervention with clients, whether individuals, families, groups, or communities.

Students are also evaluated on the degree to which they use the supervisor, pertinent others, and themselves in the learning process. This highlights the fact that students must take primary responsibility for their own learning. Interns must come to supervisory sessions prepared to discuss clients, issues, questions, and concepts. They must also demonstrate an ability to make decisions, follow-through on assignments, and know when to work independently and when to seek assistance. This includes an examination of how well the student recognizes and works through learning obstacles and the degree to which he or she recognizes areas needing development and improvement. This aspect of the evaluation process relates to the student's self-awareness.

The social work intern is also examined with regard to demonstration of commitment to the values and ethical principles of the profession. Since social work is a profession with ethical standards and a formal code of ethics, it is important that the student learn to internalize and function within the ethical principles of practice. It is recognized however that social workers are often faced with dilemmas regarding conflicting ethical issues and these matters are presented in Chapter Five.

Figure 4 - 1 illustrates a formal evaluation form. Note that the various items are related to the issues presented above.

Figure 4-1

Student Evaluation

Student_____
Date_____
Agency_____
Date of Placement_____

Briefly describe student's assignment: (Use back if necessary)

Please indicate for each of the following:
NA = Not applicable
U = Unsatisfactory
S = Satisfactory
UA = Above average
O = Outstanding

A. Agency and Community Knowledge
   The student:

   1. Demonstrates knowledge of agency purpose, structure, and functioning by appropriately using agency resources on behalf of clients and/or by discussion of these areas........ ____
   2. Seeks out information regarding agency history, policy and practice........................ ____

40

Figure 4-1 cont'd.

3. Demonstrates by discussion and activities, awareness of the agency's role in the community and its relationship to the social service network...................... ____
4. Seeks out knowledge and demonstrates appropriate use of community resources..... ____
5. Seeks out client networks.................. ____

B. Professional Goals
   The student:

1. Assumes some responsibility for learning and professional growth.................... ____
2. Treats individuals with sense of dignity and worth................................. ____
3. Exhibits empathy............................ ____
4. Exhibits understanding, awareness and acceptance of values and culture different than own.................................. ____
5. Exhibits understanding of self and own personal values and their impact on the helping process........................... ____
6. Sees possible links between client's individual problems and community and societal problems.................... ____
7. Demonstrates ability to work with and make appropriate use of colleagues......... ____
8. Understands the role and makes appropriate use of supervision........................ ____
9. Demonstrates ability to work collabora- tively with other resources including agencies, client's family and friendship network................................... ____
10. Shows understanding of advocacy and is willing to intercede on behalf of clients in various problem situations............. ____
11. Shows ability to follow through on assign- ments.................................... ____
12. Makes effective use of time and planning... ____
13. Shows initiative and motivation in tasks... ____
14. Attendance and punctuality................. ____

Figure 4-1 cont'd.

C. Knowledge/Skills
The student shows progress in development and understanding of following skills:

1. Observational.............................. ____
2. Interviewing............................... ____
3. Verbal communication....................... ____
4. Nonverbal communication.................... ____
5. Listening................................. ____
6. Recording................................. ____
7. Other writing tasks....................... ____
8. Demonstrates understanding of necessity of client participation in decision making.... ____
9. Demonstrates progressive skill in relation- ship building............................. ____
10. Exhibits knowledge and understanding of psycho-biological aspects of client........ ____
11. Shows ability to handle termination in appropriate manner........................ ____

Suggested grade: A, B+ -, C+ -, D, F.

Additional comments: (Use back if necessary).

Field Instructor_____

Student_____

Student's signature indicates the evaluation was read and does not express agreement or disagreement.

Student differences with the evaluation may be addressed here.

Date_____

Figure 4 -1 is an example of a formal evaluation document. Others may be very detailed, requiring the agency supervisor to write a more comprehensive narrative which presents the issues and items being appraised in descriptive and behavioral terms.

In the sample presented above, the supervisor is asked to suggest a letter grade for the student. Some colleges require the supervisor to assess students' performance using variations of pass - fail, satisfactory - unsatisfactory types of grading systems. A presentation of grades is included later in this chapter.

There are several formats for reporting students' performance. A detailed formal evaluation requires the supervisor to write a narrative concerning each of the several areas of student learning and development. This type of format may also include a checklist such as presented in Figure 4 - 1. The detailed formal evaluation summarizes a student's performance over some period of time, most often a semester. In this type of evaluation the student is usually required to sign the respective form indicating that he or she has read and discussed it with the supervisor.

A brief formal evaluation usually consists of a checklist and a short narrative concerning areas of interest which is completed by the supervisor and signed by the respective student. This type of format is used to note and make a record of a student's ongoing progress and is usually completed around the mid-point of the semester. Some college programs utilize the brief formal design after the student has completed a brief stay at an agency, usually four to six weeks. Thus used, the form is completed primarily to formally alert the student and school of areas of concern which may cause the student difficulty as the term and field experience progress. This type of usage also helps ensure that the student, supervisor, and college faculty share similar expectations and understanding regarding educational objectives and performance criteria early on in the learning experience.

Oral evaluation is used as an informal, ongoing communication mechanism between the supervisor and the student, supervisor and school, and student and school. Supervisory conferences can be conceptualized, in part, as representing oral evaluations. This device offers relatively quick feedback regarding student performance. Supervisors and faculty should not use the un-

documented oral evaluation to modify or change that
which has been written in more formal evaluation formats.

OTHER EVALUATION ISSUES

Student Self-Awareness

Social Work is both an art and a science. Most
students enter the profession because they like to
interact with people. They want to help others and may
have been told that they are easy to talk with and are
helpful. These personal attributes help form a basis
for professional practice; to these must be added
knowledge, skills, and disciplined use of self. There
is a difference between wanting to help others and
actually helping them; there is a difference between
being told that one is helpful by one's friends and
successfully completing a course of study in social
work.

Students who fail to realize these differences
automatically expect to be evaluated highly because of
their intentions and a less than perfect evaluation of
their performance may come as a shock to them personally. Since they are being evaluated on their conscious
use of self, they may be considerably upset by a nega-
tive evaluation of their performance. Some students may
act out their upsetment by withdrawing from the social
work program; by finding fault with the supervisor; by
attempting to complete field requirements in a per-
functionary manner; and a host of other ways. Students
who can grow and learn from the evaluation process
however are the ones who will become successful
practitioners.

The more a student is self-aware, open, and willing to assess herself and grow, the easier the evaluation process will be. Not coincidently, this is the
type of student who tends to be evaluated highly.

44

Student Self-Assessment

As part of a formal, written evaluation supervisors and colleges usually require students to complete some form of self-assessment or self-evaluation. The more analytical a student can be concerning his or her performance, the more self-aware he or she is and this is a major requirement of social work practice. Requiring the student to openly identify his strengths and weaknesses helps build self-awareness and helps form a basis for future learning and development.

There are several drawbacks to formal use of student self-assessments however. Students often feel pressure and may not have a clear perspective on their performance. If a student feels she is performing extremely well, she may not wish to evaluate herself too highly for fear the supervisor or school will think she is unrealistic. If a student feels her performance is weak in some areas, she may be hesitant to report this for fear that this may lead to a self-fulfilling prophecy regarding the formal evaluation prepared by the supervisor. A final drawback to use of student self-evaluations is that they may be used more for making the supervisor's job easier than for facilitating learning and growth. A supervisor who tells a student to write her own evaluation before she herself completes it may be trying to avoid responsibility.

Grades

The formal evaluation document helps facilitate a college grade for credits earned in the field experience. It is to be noted that the evaluation document, prepared by the supervisor in conjunction with input from the student, helps form the basis for the student's grade which is formally awarded by the college. Assigning grades to students performance is a very difficult process.

As a general rule, supervisors are not as experienced in grading as college faculty. Supervisors meet with students on a face to face basis over an extended period of time. If the student is progressing reasonably well, the supervisor may feel that A is an appropriate grade, reserving C for borderline lackluster performance, and F only when very serious problems are noted. As a result, colleges may receive an overrepresentation of A's as recommended grades from supervisors since most students progress through the field experience reasonably well. Recommending a grade of less than A at the end of one semester of the total field experience may impact on the supervisor - student relationship for the remainder of the experience, thus serving as a source of pressure on the supervisor to recommend a high grade. Students are often disappointed and upset with a grade of C, feeling that they are not performing satisfactorily even though this is what such a grade is supposed to denote.

Some colleges, recognizing the above, ask supervisors to report student performances in terms of various forms of pass/fail, satisfactory/unsatisfactory systems. While this diminishes some of the problems noted above, it may create other problems. For example, many colleges do not award pass/fail and similar grades and require that a letter or number grade be awarded to students. College faculty are then faced with the task of translating the pass/fail grade recommended by the supervisor into a letter or number grade. This requires considering and evaluating other matters and assignments applicable to the student such as submission of logs, process notes, term papers, and so forth to help form the basis for the grade.

Some colleges have provision for awarding pass/fail credit to students. This may work to the disadvantage of the outstanding student however. He or she will only have "pass" grades for a considerable number of credits while students from other college majors may have A's on their transcripts. This issue is particularly relevant to the student who wishes to enter law school or other graduate programs where undergraduate grades are key factors in the admissions process.

Some colleges offer students options between pass/fail and letter grades. While this ameliorates some of the problems noted above, it often results in the awarding of several A's, several "passes", and very few "failures" and doesn't differentiate clearly the performance of respective students.

There are a host of concerns involved with grading the performance of students and the following is presented as a guide for resolving some of these dilemmas.

The school has the final decision

regarding the grade.

The college is an accredited institution of higher learning and has responsibility for controlling the grades which appear on students' transcripts. In the event of discrepancies between the perceptions of faculty, the field supervisor, and the student, the college has ultimate responsibility. Of course, this also makes the college responsible for making serious efforts aimed at resolving disputes and discrepancies.

When in doubt, give the student

the benefit of the doubt.

Grades are important and a transcript is a permanent record. Considering such, and considering that college faculty are not infallible, it seems wise and appropriate to resolve doubts in the student's favor.

All parties involved in the field experience

should understand their role in the grading

process.

Grading is a task which is made easier and fairer by the existence of clear guidelines, honest evaluation feedback mechanisms, and the provision of ample time for reflection and discussion. Clear guidelines help ameliorate a situation whereby a student could be awarded a B by one instructor but an A by another.

There must be mechanisms for the student

to grieve or protest his or her grade.

There may be instances when a student disagrees with the grade he or she has been awarded. When a student disagrees with the supervisor's evaluation, she should first meet informally with the supervisor to see if issues and questions can be resolved. Very often, by talking things through, problems are eliminated. If informal discussions are not helpful, the student should still sign the evaluation document, noting that she has read it and also noting that she disagrees with the evaluation. The next step is for the respective faculty member, supervisor, and student to meet on a more formal basis in an attempt to resolve difficulties. It is important that this procedure be formalized since grieving an evaluation is a serious undertaking. The student should report or note her grievance as soon as possible and be prepared to present evidence and documentation of performance such as assignments, case records, records of time spent in the agency, and so forth to substantiate her position.

If this procedure does not resolve disagreements, students may be advised against pursuing a career in social work or they may be placed in another agency with another supervisor. This is a complicated process which must be reflected upon thoroughly by the student and faculty member.

Beyond the above, colleges have appeals procedures regarding students' grievances on a wide variety of matters. Students are expected to follow their respective college's formal grievance procedures. Some schools encourage and permit input from the students' peers in various stages of this process.

In addition to evaluation of the student, the field agency, supervisor, and college faculty should be evaluated by the student. Most colleges have a system for gaining feedback from students. Student evaluations of agencies and supervisors facilitate consideration of these elements for use in future semesters. They also may highlight areas where the school could be more helpful and effective in developing agencies and supervisors.

Other Evaluative and Supervisory Techniques

In addition to supervisory conferences and the review of written materials, there are several other techniques which can be helpful in evaluating students.

In some agency settings it may be possible for the supervisor to periodically be present when the student is working with a client or client group. In this manner the supervisor directly sees and hears what is transpiring. There are several drawbacks to this device which must be carefully considered however. The presence of the supervisor may result in both the client and student feeling especially self-conscious or guarded, thus defeating the purpose of the supervisor's presence. The presence of a third party may stifle the natural communication flow between the student and client and both may feel awkward, uneasy, or anxious. This is especially problematic considering that clients come to agencies for help, not to facilitate students' learning. The client's permission should be secured before a third party may be present.

A less awkward method of observing the student is for the student and supervisor to share responsibilities for working with a client or client group. This arrangement should be presented to clients during the contracting phase of the helping process. This type of arrangement requires careful planning regarding the roles and responsibilities of the student and supervisor, with consideration for the client's presenting problem and ability to work with more than one person at the agency.

The one-way mirror is another observational tool for evaluating the student. Unless there are very good reasons for the contrary, permission of clients is to be obtained before using this device. Even if permission is granted, care must be taken to monitor the effect of the one-way mirror on the client. Again, clients come to agencies for help, not to facilitate students learning.

Use of an audio tape recorder is another means of obtaining feedback about a student's performance. Of course, one can only hear voices and not see the affective responses of the student and client. Still, the audio tape recorder can be helpful in giving a sense of the student's communication skills, particularly those related to beginning and ending interviews, questioning, and listening. How the student deals with silence or humor can also be revealed in a tape recording. Taping can also enable the student to listen and critique herself subsequent to the interview. As with supervisor observation/participation and one-way mirror viewing, clients must grant permission to be recorded. Some client situations may not be appropriate for taping, particularly those client situations which have legal implications, such as helping a parent avoid abusing a child.

In using the tape recorder the client and the student at first may feel self-conscious about what is said, however as time passes its presence may become less and less an issue of concern to them. The student must carefully assess the degree to which the presence of a tape recorder impedes a client's ability or willingness to openly communicate.

The use of video taping has opened a new dimension for observing student/client interactions. The supervisor and student can watch and listen to a tape repeatedly in an effort to evaluate the student's verbal and non-verbal performance and make suggestions for improvement. Video taping, however, is an obtrusive devise. Additional lighting is usually required and it is hard to avoid being conscious of the camera. Another drawback to this device is its relatively high expense. Agencies, particularly smaller ones, would prefer to expend funds for providing services to clients.

As presented in this chapter, evaluation is a difficult process. Knowing what to evaluate; establishing performance criteria to be used as a basis for evaluation; providing practice experiences in areas to be evaluated and; establishing mechanisms to help substantiate the evaluation are tasks requiring considerable thought and dedication on the part of students, supervisors, and faculty.

REFERENCES

1. Kerrigan, Irene: The Field Instructor as Social Work Educator. New York, Columbia University Press, 1978, p. 63.

2. Wilson, Suanna: Field Instruction. New York, The Free Press, 1981, p. 164.

Chapter Five

Ethics and Social Work

The field experience is designed to expose students to ethical social work practice and give them opportunities to act in accordance with the values of the profession. Social workers hold the following beliefs:

> The environment (social, physical, organizational) should provide the opportunity and resources for the maximum realization of the potential and aspirations of all individuals, for their common human needs, and for the alleviation of distress and suffering;

> Individuals should contribute as effectively as they can to their own well-being and to the social welfare of others in their immediate environment as well as the collective society;

> Transactions between individuals and others in their environment should enhance the dignity, individuality, and self-determination of everyone. People should be treated humanely and with justice. (1)

At the lowest level of learning, students might be asked on an examination to state what social workers believe. In this instance, a student would merely have to memorize the preceding. At a somewhat higher level of learning, students might be asked to state the beliefs of social workers, using their own words and explicating examples. Answering questions such as these is typical of many college courses in a host of subject areas.

In the field experience however, students must demonstrate by their actions that they understand and have internalized the belief system of social work. In other words, beliefs and values must be transformed into professional practice.

51

Beliefs and values are the foundation upon which knowledge, skills, and techniques are built. They are the principles for ethical conduct. As is typical of most professions, social work has incorporated these principles for ethical behavior into a Code of Ethics. In 1979, the Delegate Assembly of the National Association of Social Workers (NASW) revised the profession's Code of Ethics (2) and this is presented at the conclusion of this chapter.

NON-JUDGEMENTAL ATTITUDE

There are several major guides which enables social workers to conduct themselves in an ethical manner and be of service to clients.(3) One such guide is the notion that they must have a non-judgemental attitude. Being non-judgemental means keeping an open mind; recognizing that each individual attempts to deal with their life circumstances in the best way they know how. This does not mean that social workers do not make judgements. On the contrary, forming opinions and making assessments are key components of the helping process. In addition, a non-judgemental attitude does not mean that social workers condone antisocial or destructive activities. Non-judgementalism refers to a state of mind in which professionals accept people as individuals who deserve respect and who should be treated with dignity. While a social worker may not agree personally with a client's life-style or beliefs, he does accept the client as a unique individual who is to be welcomed into the helping process.

It cannot be emphasized strongly enough that having a non-judgemental attitude is easier said than done. There are strong psychological and social forces acting upon each of us, telling us that our way of behaving and thinking are the most correct. Being non-judgemental involves consciously trying to understand another persons's perspective without being quite so quick to judge that person as somehow in error, as might be more typical of those who are untrained in this area.

Being non-judgemental is a difficult process throughout one's career. It may be a harder learning experience for people who have experienced some social problem themselves and who subsequently work with people who are experiencing a similar problem. For example, consider a beginning practitioner who has grown up in poverty and who overcomes a host of obstacles, graduates college, and becomes a social worker in an anti-poverty program. This social worker may have to work especially hard at not being self-righteous ("I made it because I worked hard. These people must be lazy.")

Social work students must learn to consciously have an accepting attitude and must learn to convey this to clients in what they say and do, including their voice inflections and subtle body language messages. A good point to remember is that social workers exist to help people, not to judge them.

To illustrate the above, consider a social worker in a hospital where it has been medically assessed that a seventy-five year old patient no longer requires acute medical care but who cannot function independently in her own apartment either. This type of assessment is based on the judgements of members of the health care team - doctors, nurses, social workers, physical therapists, and others. Based on these judgements, it is decided that the patient might be able to return to the community if her daughter would take her into her own home, otherwise placement in a nursing home seems the only viable alternative.

In this particular hospital, discharge planning is the responsibility of the social worker. This particular social worker, based on her own experiences, personally feels strongly that family members are responsible for each other at all costs and that nursing homes should be the exception rather than the rule for many of those who are frail, elderly, and have medical problems.

The social worker meets with the patient who states she would like to live with her daughter. The worker must be very careful to not give the patient a message that this is the best decision because she does not have enough information. Subsequently, the social worker meets with the patient's daughter who reports that she has her own family and job and cannot care for her mother in her own home. This is a typical problem in medical social work practice. The social worker must be careful not to react to the patient's daughter in a judgemental manner. She must be self-aware of her own feelings regarding the care of infirm senior citizens so as not to impose her values on the daughter. The social worker must consciously avoid feeling that people like the daughter are cold, insensitive, or non-caring. After all, she knows little about the daughter's life circumstances.

This illustration represents one of several typical dilemmas (4) in social work practice - who is the client? Is the hospital the client? It is paying the social worker's salary to implement discharge plans for those who no longer require acute medical care. Is the patient a client? Clearly, the patient is a client. The social worker's responsibility transcends merely determining the patient's wishes. She must work with the patient to arrive at a realistic, acceptable plan for her future care. Is the daughter a client? The worker's role transcends merely asking the daughter to take the patient to her home. She must work with her as well to arrive at a realistic, acceptable plan.

CLIENT SELF-DETERMINATION

Another major guide to ethical practice is the notion of client self-determination. In working with clients our professional role is to help them develop their own capacities for decision-making and maximum social functioning. The basic premise is that, ultimately, people have the right to make their own decisions and not have decisions imposed upon them. It is to be noted, again, that social workers do not condone anti-social or destructive behaviors. One would not apply the principle of self-determination to a mother who wishes to use her five year old son in the making of pornography.

Using client self-determination as a guide to practice is a difficult process requiring patience, time, training, and experience. Quite often, clients perceive us as experts and come to us seeking our advice. The social work intern must keep in mind that social workers very rarely give advice; our professional role is to help people increase their own capacities for decision-making. Social work is not mere advice-giving or counseling, it is a complicated helping process. A social work novice may be tempted to provide a client with the "one best answer" because she wants to be helpful or to meet her own needs for being perceived as an "expert". This type of thinking must consciously be avoided.

Consider a nineteen year old college student who is pregnant and unmarried. She meets with a social worker and asks "What should I do?". The social worker must keep in mind that, ultimately, the client knows what is best for herself. She must realize that people often do not have sufficient information upon which to make decisions. The social worker is responsible for providing the client with information about potential options and helping the client understand the possible consequences of each.

An impediment to the simple application of the principle of self-determination is ambivalence. Very often clients can be overwhelmed by problems, information, consequences, and so forth that the result is ambivalence; an inability or unwillingness to make decisions or take action. This is one example of why social work is a helping process which transcends the mere giving of advice and information. Social workers are responsible for recognizing ambivalence and helping clients to overcome it.

As with issues that violate the law or which contradict major social norms, there are circumstances under which the principle of self-determination cannot be indiscriminately applied. There are people who, for reasons such as their young age or mental status, cannot reasonably be expected to have high level capacities for making decisions. In some instances the social worker may have to assume a caretaker role insofar as meeting the needs of these types of clients. It must be noted however that this type of activity is the exception, rather than the rule, in professional social work practice.

The social work student, as well as experienced practitioners, must keep in mind that there are institutionalized blockages to self-determination. If social institutions function in a way which somehow discriminates against people based on social class, race, sex, or age, this reduces the options various categories of people have regarding these institutions. Consequently, the professional organization of social workers has as one of its goals the elimination of these types of discrimination.

Serving and helping others is a complicated process involving conscious, life-long learning. Clients are not interested in our intentions as much as they are interested in results. As a guide for practice, the National Association of Social Workers has articulated a Code of Ethics which is presented with their permission.

PREAMBLE

This code is intended to serve as a guide to the everyday conduct of members of the social work profession and as a basis for the adjudication of issues in ethics when the conduct of social workers is alleged to deviate from the standards expressed or implied in this code. It represents standards of ethical behavior for social workers in professional relationships with those served, with colleagues, with employers, with other individuals and professions, and with the community and society as a whole. It also embodies standards of ethical behavior governing individual conduct to the extent that such conduct is associated with an individual's status and identity as a social worker.

This code is based on the fundamental values of the social work profession that include the worth, dignity, and uniqueness of all persons as well as their rights and opportunities. It is also based on the nature of social work, which fosters conditions that promote these values.

In subscribing to and abiding by this code, the social worker is expected to view ethical responsibility in as inclusive a context as each situation demands and within which ethical judgement is required. The social worker is expected to take into consideration all the principles in this code that have a bearing upon any situation in which ethical judgement is to be exercised and professional intervention or conduct is planned. The course of action that the social worker chooses is expected to be consistent with the spirit as well as the letter of this code.

In itself, this code does not represent a set of rules that will prescribe all the behaviors of social workers in all the complexities of professional life. Rather, it offers general principles to guide conduct, and the judicious appraisal of conduct, in situations that have ethical implications. It provides the basis for making judgments about ethical actions before and after they occur. Frequently, the particular situation determines the ethical principles that apply and the manner of their application. In such cases, not only the particular principles are taken into immediate consideration, but also the entire code and its spirit. Specific applications of ethical principles must be judged within the context in which they are being considered. Ethical behavior in a given situation must satisfy not only the judgment of the individual social worker, but also the judgement of an unbiased jury of professional peers.

This code should not be used as an instrument to deprive any social worker of the opportunity or freedom to practice with complete professional integrity; nor should any disciplinary action be taken on the basis of this code without maximum provision for safeguarding the rights of the social worker affected.

The ethical behavior of social workers results not from edict, but from a personal commitment of the individual. This code is offered to affirm the will and zeal of all social workers to be ethical and to act ethically in all that they do as social workers.

The following codified ethical principles should guide social workers in the various roles and relationships and at the various levels of responsibility in which they function professionally. These principles also serve as a basis for the adjudication by the National Association of Social Workers of issues in ethics. In subscribing to this code, social workers are required to cooperate in its implementation and abide by any disciplinary rulings based on it. They should also take adequate measures to discourage, prevent, expose, and correct the unethical conduct of colleagues. Finally, social workers should be equally ready to defend and assist colleagues unjustly charged with unethical conduct.

I. The Social Worker's Conduct and Comportment as a Social Worker
   A. Propriety--The social worker should maintain high standards of personal conduct in the capacity or identity as social worker.
      1. The private conduct of the social worker is a personal matter to the same degree as is any other person's, except when such conduct compromises the fulfillment of professional responsibilities.
      2. The social worker should not participate in, condone, or be associated with dishonesty, fraud, deceit, or misrepresentation.
      3. The social worker should distinguish clearly between statements and actions made as a private individual and as a representative of the social work profession or an organization or group.

   B. Competence and Professional Development--The social worker should strive to become and remain proficient in professional practice and the performance of professional functions.

      1. The social worker should accept responsibility or employment only on the basis of existing competence or the intention to acquire the necessary competence.
      2. The social worker should not misrepresent professional qualifications, education, experience, or affiliations.

   C. Service--The social worker should regard as primary the service obligation of the social work profession.

      1. The social worker should retain ultimate responsibility for the quality and extent of the service that the individual assumes, assigns, or performs.
      2. The social worker should act to prevent practices that are inhumane or discriminatory against any person or group of persons.

   D. Integrity--The social worker should act in accordance with the highest standards of professional integrity and impartiality.

      1. The social worker should be alert to and resist the influences and pressures that interfere with the exercise of professional

discretion and impartial judgement required
for the performance of professional functions.
2. The social worker should not exploit professional relationships for personal gain.

E. Scholarship and Research--The social worker
engaged in study and research should be guided
by the conventions of scholarly inquiry.
1. The social worker engaged in research should
consider carefully its possible consequences
for human beings.
2. The social worker engaged in research should
ascertain that the consent of participants in
the research is voluntary and informed, without any implied deprivation or penalty for
refusal to participate, and with due regard
for participants' privacy and dignity.
3. The social worker engaged in research should
protect participants from unwarranted
physical or mental discomfort, distress,
harm, danger, or deprivation.
4. The social worker who engages in the
evaluation of services or cases should
discuss them only for professional purposes
and only with persons directly and
professionally concerned with them.
5. Information obtained about participants in
research should be treated as confidential.
6. The social worker should take credit only for
work actually done in connection with
scholarly and research endeavors and credit
contributions made by others.

II. The Social Worker's Ethical Responsibility to
Clients
F. Primacy of Clients' Interests--The social
worker's primary responsibility is to clients.
1. The social worker should serve clients with
devotion, loyalty, determination, and the
maximum application of professional skill and
competence.
2. The social worker should not exploit relationships with clients for personal
advantage, or solicit the clients of one's
agency for private practice.
3. The social worker should not practice,
condone, facilitate or collaborate with any
form of discriminination on the basis of
race, color, sex, sexual orientation, age,
religion, national origin, marital status,

59

political belief, mental or physical handicap, or any other preference or personal characteristic, condition or status.
4. The social worker should avoid relationships or commitments that conflict with the interests of clients.
5. The social worker should under no circumstances engage in sexual activities with clients.
6. The social worker should provide clients with accurate and complete information regarding the extent and nature of the services available to them.
7. The social worker should appraise clients of their risks, rights, opportunities, and obligations associated with social service to them.
8. The social worker should seek advice and counsel of colleagues and supervisors whenever such consultation is in the best interest of clients.
9. The social worker should terminate service to clients and professional relationships with them, when such service and relationships are no longer required or no longer serve the clients' needs or interests.
10. The social worker should withdraw services precipitously only under unusual circumstances, giving careful consideration to all factors in the situation and taking care to minimize possible adverse effects.
11. The social worker who anticipates the termination or interruption of service to clients should notify clients promptly and seek the transfer, referral, or continuation of service in relation to the clients' needs and preferences.

G. Rights and Prerogatives of Clients--The social worker should make every effort to foster maximum self-determination on the part of clients.
1. When the social worker must act on behalf of a client who has been adjudged legally imcompetent, the social worker should safeguard the interests and rights of that client.
2. When another individual has been legally authorized to act on behalf of a client, the social worker should deal with that person always with the client's best interest in mind.

3. The social worker should not engage in any action that violates or diminishes the civil or legal rights of clients.

H. Confidentiality and Privacy--The social worker should respect the privacy of clients and hold in confidence all information obtained in the course of professional service.
   1. The social worker should not share with others confidences revealed by clients, without their consent, and then only for compelling professional reasons.
   2. The social worker should inform clients fully about the limits of confidentiality in a given situation, the purposes for which information is obtained, and how it may be used.
   3. The social worker should afford clients reasonable access to any official social work records concerning them.
   4. When providing clients with access to records, the social worker should take due care to protect the confidences of others contained in those records.
   5. The social worker should obtain informed consent of clients before taping, recording, or permitting third party observation of their activities.

I. Fees--When setting fees, the social worker should ensure that they are fair, reasonable, considerate and commensurate with the service performed and with due regard for the clients' ability to pay.
   1. The social worker should not divide a fee or accept or give anything of value for receiving or making a referral.

III. The Social Worker's Ethical Responsibility to Colleagues
J. Respect, Fairness, and Courtesy--The social worker should treat colleagues with respect, courtesy, fairness, and good faith.
   1. The social worker should cooperate with colleagues to promote professional interests and concerns.
   2. The social worker should respect confidence shared by colleagues in the course of their professional relationships and transactions.
   3. The social worker should create and maintain conditions of practice that facilitate ethi-

61

cal and competent professional performance by colleagues.

4. The social worker should treat with respect, and represent accurately and fairly, the qualifications, views, and findings of colleagues and use appropriate channels to express judgements on these matters.

5. The social worker who replaces or is replaced by a colleague in professional practice should act with consideration for the interest, character, and reputation of that colleague.

6. The social worker should not exploit a dispute between a colleague and employers to obtain a position or otherwise advance the social worker's interest.

7. The social worker should seek arbitration or mediation when conflicts with colleagues require resolution for compelling professional reasons.

8. The social worker should extend to colleagues of other professions the same respect and cooperation that is extended to social work colleagues.

9. The social worker who serves as an employer, supervisor, or mentor to colleagues should make orderly and explicit arrangements regarding the conditions of their continuing professional relationship.

10. The social worker who has the responsibility for employing and evaluating the performance of other staff members, should fulfill such responsibility in a fair, considerate, and equitable manner, on the basis of clearly enunciated criteria.

11. The social worker who has the responsibility for evaluating the performance of employees, supervisees, or students should share evaluations with them.

K. Dealing with Colleagues' Clients--The social worker has the responsibility to relate to the clients of colleagues with full professional consideration.

1. The social worker should not solicit the clients of colleagues.

2. The social worker should not assume professional responsibility for the clients of another agency or a colleague without appropriate communication with that agency or colleague.

3. The social worker who serves the clients of colleagues during a temporary absence or emergency, should serve those clients with the same consideration as that afforded any client.

IV. The Social Worker's Ethical Responsibility to Employers and Employing Organizations.

L. Commitment to Employing Organization--The social worker should adhere to commitments made to the employing organization.
   1. The social worker should work to improve the employing agency's policies and procedures, and the efficiency and effectiveness of its services.
   2. The social worker should not accept employment or arrange student field placements in an organization which is currently under public sanction by NASW for violating personnel standards or imposing limitations on behalf of clients.
   3. The social worker should act to prevent and eliminate discrimination in the employing organization's work assignments and in its employment policies and practices.
   4. The social worker should use with scrupulous regard and only for the purpose for which they are intended the resources of the employing organization.

V. The Social Worker's Ethical Responsibility to the Social Work Profession

M. Maintaining the Integrity of the Profession--The social worker should uphold and advance the values, ethics, knowledge, and mission of the profession.
   1. The social worker should protect and enhance the dignity and integrity of the profession and should be responsible and vigorous in discussion and criticism of the profession.
   2. The social worker should take action through appropriate channels against unethical conduct by any other member of the profession.
   3. The social worker should act to prevent the unauthorized and unqualified practice of social work.
   4. The social worker should make no misrepresentation in advertising as to qualifications, competence, service, or results to

63

be achieved.

N. Community Service--The social worker should assist the profession in making social services available to the general public.
1. The social worker should contribute time and professional expertise to activities that promote respect for the utility, the integrity, and the competence of the social work profession.
2. The social worker should support the formulation, development, enactment and implementation of social policies of concern to the profession.

O. Development of Knowledge--The social worker should take responsibility for identifying, developing, and fully utilizing knowledge for professional practice.
1. The social worker should base practice upon recognized knowledge relevant to social work.
2. The social worker should critically examine, and keep current with, emerging knowledge relevant to social work.
3. The social worker should contribute to the knowledge base of social work and share research knowledge and practice wisdom with colleagues.

VI. The Social Worker's Ethical Responsibility to Society
P. Promoting the General Welfare--The social worker should promote the general welfare of society.
1. The social worker should act to prevent and eliminate discrimination against any person or group on the basis of race, color, sex, sexual orientation, age, religion, national origin, marital status, political belief, mental or physical handicap, or any other preference or personal characteristic, condition, or status.
2. The social worker should act to ensure that all persons have access to the resources, services, and opportunities which they require.
3. The social worker should act to expand choice and opportunity for all persons, with special regard for disadvantaged or oppressed groups and persons.

4. The social worker should promote conditions that encourage respect for the diversity of cultures which constitute American society.

5. The social worker should provide appropriate professional services in public emergencies.
6. The social worker should advocate changes in policy and legislation to improve social conditions and to promote social justice.
7. The social worker should encourage informed participation by the public in shaping social policies and institutions.

REFERENCES

1. Working statement on the purpose of social work. Social Work, 26: 6 January 1981.

2. NASW News, Vol. 25, No. 1, January 1980, pp. 25-26.

3. Blake, Richard: Social Work: A Rewarding Career. Springfield, Ill., Charles C. Thomas Publ., 1982, Chapter 3. With contributions by Phylis J. Peterman.

4. Loewenberg, Frank and Dolgoff, Ralph: Ethical Decisions for Social Work Practice. Itasca, Ill., F.E. Peacock, 1982.

Index